new orleans

W9-CYB-702

eat.shop new orleans was researched by:
bonnie markel and dave mead

photographed by dave mead

written by: bonnie markel and dave mead
with additional writing by:
todd van horne, tracy proler and
robert, diane and gabriel markel

about eat.shop new orleans

usually in this section, i would talk a bit about the *eat.shop guides* in general. but the new orleans guide is a bit special as it's a book that celebrates what once was and still is vibrant in this most vibrant of cities: the eating and the shopping.

let's go back in time two years. it was august 2005, and i was finalizing the spring production for the guides. at the top of the list was new orleans. plans were being made to begin production on the book when katrina hit. i watched the tragedy unfold from my safe vantage point in portland, oregon, and felt helpless. i went to sleep each night mourning for the people of new orleans. each day i woke and wondered what could i do to help that would go beyond giving money or getting in a car and heading for the south to volunteer.

and then one day, almost a year after the storm, i received an email from a man named michael mott. he wrote to me about the retail business he worked for in nola called *shoefty*. he wrote so eloquently about his and sarah's (the owner of *shoefty*) love of new orleans and how they wanted to stay and fight for its survival, and how many of the local business owners also weren't giving up. after talking to michael, i knew what my role could be in nola's recovery: i could put *eat.shop new orleans* back in production.

not soon after i made the decision, my friend marianne, who co-authors *eat.shop austin* with me, told me about her friend bonnie markel and her husband dave mead. when she told me about bonnie's family's deep roots in the city, i knew she was perfect for the job and she just happened to be married to a guy who not only takes great pictures but has a serious passion for his wife's hometown.

so this is our love letter to the big easy and its absolutely spectacular eating and shopping establishments. i urge you to not only book your ticket now and re-visit this true gem of an american city, but to support the businesses featured here and all of the other local businesses in the city, both big and small. and if you can't physically visit, then remember that many of these businesses, like the *idea factory* and *southern candymakers,* have websites and that gift-buying online supports them also!

here are a couple of things to remember when visiting nola:

• make sure to double check the hours of the business before you go by calling or visiting their websites. often the businesses change their hours seasonally.

• the pictures and descriptions of each business are representational. please don't be distraught when the business no longer carries or is not serving something you saw or read about in the guide.

• if you're visiting the city, we know you'll need a rest eventually. so we've listed some of our favorite hotels on a following page to help you make your choice.

• yes, nola has crime. but so does every other city that the eat.shop guides feature. so use your noggin and don't go walking down french quarter's dark alleys at three a.m. after drinking five hurricanes.

help to revitalize new orleans: eat. shop. enjoy!

kaie wellman > publisher, *eat.shop guides* > kaie@eatshopguides.com

bonnie and dave's notes on new orleans

first thing I'd like to do is offer up a quick history reminder in case you've forgotten how important the city of nola (read: new orleans) is to the fabric of this country. ok, so it goes like this: the french claim ownership, then cede to the spanish. then the french take claim once again. then l'il ol' napolean sells us this piece of real estate. and then the british try unsuccessfully to take it from us. and then there's an influx of americans and french folk and the city doubles in size almost overnight. and then the north and south draw a line in the sand (sorta). and then the union captures new orleans (probably because the south was enjoying itself) early during the war between the states, thus, saving the city from major destruction. thus, encrypting nola with architecture and history and culture and flavor and so forth. levees are built, jazz is born, rouxs are stirred, cocktails are created, mardi gras floats are decorated, a pro football team is formed. and then, as led zeppelin predicted, the levees broke. catastrophic and heartwrenching? yes. enough to sink the city? hardly.

having grown up in houston, i've always felt a deep connection to my bayou brethren down the interstate. sure they talk a bit funny and sure they dance to the beat of a different drummer, but the folks of new orleans know how to live. so before kaie wellman could even finish asking us if we wanted to author the *eat.shop.new orleans* book, my wife bonnie and i were halfway to the big easy. bonnie grew up in new orleans and her family is seven generations deep in residency. her family lost everything in the flood, everything but a rock solid love for the city and a desire to do their part to rebuild what is arguably one of the most treasured, most historical, most cultural, most important cities in this great country of ours. and i can't help but think that every time bonnie and i visit new orleans, whether it be for the holidays, jazzfest, mardi gras or simply a weekend getaway, we're doing our part to bring the city back to its feet. and on its feet it's standing. if you're going, you might find that operating hours of certain shops and restaurants have been adjusted. but, for the most part, new orleans is probably just as you remember it. vibrant and raucous. infrastructure is intact, streetcars are running, cabs are aplenty.

we'd like to thank a few special folks for helping sculpt this literary mashed-potato-volcano of a guidebook. for starters, the markel family—bonnie's father, robert, her mother, dianne and her brother, gabriel. without them, this book wouldn't have been possible. they live, breathe, eat and shop all things nola. while making this book, they housed us, navigated us and fueled our fire for finding the best places in town. seven generations deep, the markels own and operate a 75-year-old lumberyard. needless to say, they're doing their part to rebuild the city, one two-by-four at a time. in addition to the markels, we'd like to thank creative writers and new orleans revelers, todd van horne and tracy proler. these dear friends helped us uncover some of the best new orleans has to offer. born in germany, raised all over, new orleans was the first city todd ever fell in love with. since the start of his college days, he visited often and fantasized daily about living in the big easy. rational thoughts soon took over and todd could do nothing but love nola from afar, while being jealous of those who lived there. as for tracy, before she was even so much as an inkling of her father's imagination or an apple of her mother's eye, she would make new orleans a piece of her eternal history and origin... literally. it was a fateful evening in 1972 when her parents went to see the thoroughbreds run at the fairgrounds, had a few mint juleps at the jockey club and then went out for some smooth n'awlins-style music, and that was all she wrote. nine months later tracy was added to the long list of this city's many devotees and was truly born to help us write this book.

so geaux eat. geaux shop. geaux nola.

bonnie markel and dave mead > bonnie@eatshopguides.com

more notes on new orleans

each of the businesses in this book have a little blurb written about them. each of these is written by the people noted on the previous page, and they are identified as such—d: dave, b: bonnie, tvh: todd van horne, t: tracy, di: dianne, r: robert, g: gabriel.

here are some great things to do in nola other than eating and shopping:

1> the cemeteries: new orleans has city blocks (whole neighborhoods, really) of above-ground cemeteries, or cities of the dead, which are rich in local history and make for interesting photographs.

2> garden district architecture: take a walking tour of this oak tree lined historic sector of town. see everything from queen anne victorians to classic greek revivals and italianate villas. this neighborhood is the essence of new orleans elegance and sophistication.

3> audubon park and zoo: named after painter john james audubon and designed by john olmsted, nephew of famed frederick olmsted, new york city's central park creator. walk, play, golf or just sit and admire the mighty mississippi.

4> river road plantation tours: the history of louisiana comes to life along this stretch of land. the sprawling antebellum plantations and gardens are rich in history and some are even haunted. make note: you can stay over night at a few of these amazing landmarks.

5> louisiana swamps: you should try to visit the swamps and wetlands if time permits; gators, cajun fishermen and pirogues (small, flat-bottomed boats) abound.

and finally, everybody knows that new orleans has some of the best bars and live music around, here are some of our favorite entertainment spots:

jean lafitte's blacksmith shop
rock-n-bowl
pal's lounge
carousel piano bar and lounge at the monteleone hotel
mimi's
molly's on the market
columns hotel bar
tipitina's
f & m's (late night after 2am)

and one more thing. a couple of our favorite spots had still not re-opened when we were working on the book—but make sure to check in on them because they might be opened now : dooky chase restaurant, willie mae's scotch house and camellia grill.

the master list, neighborhoods and map info

uptown
<carrollton ave to washington ave. tchoupitoulas st to willow st>
eat:
alberta
casamentos
clancy's
dick & jenny's
hansen's sno-bliz
joey k's
la boulangerie
la crêpe nanou
la petite grocery
lilette
o'delice french bakery
roman candy man
st james cheese company
savvy gourmet
sucré
shop:
angelique baby
as you like it silver shop
bamboo apothecary
belladonna
bellanoche
dominique giordano
hazelnut
n.o. surf shop
neophobia
pied nu
ropa fashion loft
scriptura
shoefty
spring
style lab
sweet pea & tulip boutique
uptown costume and dancewear

french quarter
<fn.rampart to the river. canal st to esplanade st>
eat:
bayona
café du monde
central grocery co.
croissant d'or patisserie
el gato negro
napoleon house
southern candymakers
verti marte
shop:
a gallery of fine photography
bottom of the barrel antiques
fleur de paris
hové
idea factory
le garage
louisiana loom works
louisiana music factory
meilleur joaillerie
quarter past time
serendipitous masks
the kite shop jackson square
the sword and the pen

mid city
<tulane ave to esplanade ave n. & s. claiborne to i-10>
eat:
angelo brocato's
café degas
fairgrinds coffeehouse
la vita
liuzza's by the track
lola's
mandina's
mchardy's
parkway bakery & tavern
shop:
lux
swirl

jefferson
<river rd to jefferson hwy monticello to clearview>
eat:
crabby jack's

warehouse district
<poydras st to hwy 90. carondelet st to the river>
eat:
cochon
crescent city farmers market
herbsaint
shop:
le mieux galleries
new orleans artworks
w.i.n.o.

cbd (central business district)
<poydras st to canal st. i-10 to the river>
eat:
liborio

riverbend
<monticello to broadway. the river to s. claiborne>
eat:
brigtsen's
jacques-imo's cafe
iris
mat & naddie's
shop:
angelique and victoria's
eclectic home
yvonne la fleur

bywater
<franklin to industrial canal n. rampart st. to the river>
eat:
elizabeth's
feelings café
the joint

lower garden district
<washington ave to hwy 90. st. charles ave to the river>
eat:
café reconcile
surrey's café and juice bar
shop:
aidan gill for men
house of lounge
la bella nouvelle orleans
southern fossil & mineral exchange

treme
<n. rampart to n.claiborne esplanade ave to canal st.>
eat:
li'l dizzy's cafe

(maps)

because we wanted to give you the most detailed maps possible, our city maps are now available on line. please go to:

http://maps.eatshopguides.com/nola/

here you will find a map of the entire city, with indicators showing where each business is.

bookmark this url into your pda, and you'll have the mapping data right with you as you explore.

if you don't own a pda, but want a great street map of the city, the eat.shop authors love the *streetwise* maps. they are indispensable tools when you need a take-along map with lots of detail.

where to rest your weary head

here are a few of our favorite places to stay in new orleans:

soniat house
1133 chartres street
800.544.8808 / www.soniathouse.com
standard double from $240.00
notes: small luxury hotel nestled in the historic french quarter

loft 523
523 gravier street
504.200.6523 / www.loft523.com
loft deluxe from $140.00
bars: loft523 bar and grotto room
notes: sophisticated, urban sanctuary

international house
221 camp street
800.633.5770 / www.ihhotel.com
deluxe queen from $99.00
bar: loa bar
notes: contemporary boutique hotel

hotel monteleone
214 royal street
www.hotelmonteleone.com
standard deluxe: from $149.00
restaurants: hunt room grill and le café
bar: carousel piano bar & lounge
notes: timeless historic hotel

and a couple more suggestions:
the ritz carlton new orleans (www.ritzcarlton.com/en/properties/neworleans)
w new orleans (www.starwoodhotels.com/whotels/neworleans)
intercontinental new orleans (www.new-orleans.intercontinental.com/)

bonnie & dave's twenty favorite things

01 > seafood platter (aka shellfish diet) at brigtsen's

02 > slow-roasted duck po'boy at crabby jack's

03 > lava flow at hansen's sno-bliz

04 > carrot margarita at el gato negro

05 > crab salad from alberta

06 > praline bacon from elizabeth's

07 > stewed rabbit and dumplings from cochon

08 > bread pudding from li'l dizzy's

09 > peanut butter pie from feelings cafe

10 > chandeliers from meilleur joaillerie

11 > the shave at aidan gill for men

12 > zac posen handbags from shoefty

13 > whirligigs and flip tops from idea factory

14 > red flower pedicure from bamboo apothecary

15 > russian demitasse set from as you like it silver shop

16 > handmade derby hat from fleur de paris

17 > orange '60s mod lamps from neophobia

18 > pre-civil war perfume bottle from the sword and pen

19 > peculiar pair press stationary from scriptura

20 > matta poofs from pied nu

notes

notes

alberta

fine dining in a relaxed atmosphere

5015 magazine street. between robert and soniat
504. 891.3015
tue - sat 6 - 11p

opened in 2005. owner: alberta pate chef: melody pate
$$ - $$$: all major credit cards accepted
dinner. full bar. reservations recommended

uptown > **e01**

tvh: the feeling you get immediately at *alberta* is that it's cozy and warm. the best way i can describe it is that it's just like being at the house you grew up in, except your sister is a world-class chef and your mom puts gorgeous linens on all the furniture. along with the cozy warmth, there's an elegance here that makes me think that this is the perfect place to propose marriage—but make sure to order the rosé champagne and to eat some crab salad. it will have your beloved primed to say yes. oh, and by the way... make sure to ask her dad.

imbibe / devour:
bruno paillard rosé premiere cuvee champagne
paraiso santa lucia highlands pinot noir
amazing crab salad
escargot with gnocchi & mushroom ragout
scallops with pea shoots & orange butter sauce
sweetbreads with rosti potatoes & garlic marsala
saffron mussels

11

angelo brocato ice cream & confectionary

specializing in italian ice cream and pastries

214 north carrollton avenue. between iberville and bienville
504.486.0078 www.angelobrocatoicecream.com
tue - thu 10a - 10p fri - sat 10a - 10:30p sun 10a - 9p

opened in 1905. owner: arthur brocato
$: all major credit cards accepted
coffee / tea. treats

mid city >

ROMAN CANDY 75¢
each

b: i scream, you scream, we all scream for italian ice cream... and with good reason at *angelo brocato's ice cream & confectionary*. if you haven't ever eaten their italian ice or spumoni, you're missing out. this place is an institution, and they have a hundred years under their belt to prove it. markets have collapsed, wars have been fought and levees have been broken, but one thing has been a mainstay in the big easy: *brocato's*. so put your worries behind you, relax and enjoy. the weight of the world will feel a bit lighter after a few bites of *brocato's* lemon italian ice.

imbibe / devour:
ices:
  blood orange
  lemon italian
  strawberry italian
chestnut gelato
spumoni
cannoli (made fresh while you wait)
cucidata (italian fig cookies)

bayona

eclectic global cuisine
430 dauphine street. between st. louis and conti
504.525.4455 www.bayona.com
lunch wed - fri 11:30a - til close sat noon - 3p dinner mon - sat 6p - til close

opened in 1990. owner: regina keever chef/co-owner: susan spicer
$$ - $$$: all major credit cards accepted
lunch (sat lite lunch). dinner. full bar. reservations recommended

french quarter > **e03**

d: should elvis aaron presley return from the dead, my bet is that he'd gyrate his wide hips straight to *bayona* and ask for a table for one. i can't be certain that susan spicer, chef and co-founder of *bayona* is or was a fan of the king but with a smoked duck, cashew butter and pepper jelly sandwich on the lunch menu, my guess is that she can name at least ten of his eighteen billboard number one hits. i can name all eighteen. with cashew butter stuck to the roof of my mouth.

imbibe / devour:
04 valpolicella classico superiore, mazzi, veneto
02 schramsberg blanc de noir sparkling wine
chilled cucumber soup with salmon & dill tartare
sweetbreads with potatoes, mushrooms & mustard
peppered lamb loin with herbed goat cheese
    & zinfandel sauce
creole cream cheese cannoli with blackberries
    & lemon thyme syrup

brigtsen's

rebuilding new orleans one delicious plate at a time

723 dante street. corner of maple
504.861.7610 www.brigtsens.com
tue - sat 5:30 - 10p

opened in 1986. owner / chef: frank brigtsen   co-owner: marna brigtsen
$$$: all major credit cards accepted
dinner. full bar. reservations recommended

riverbend >

d: my wife bonnie's in the dog house. and her parents are too. why? they're new orleans natives, and they've never taken me to *brigtsen's* until now. i've spent a lot of time in the big easy and i have some favorite restaurants, but this place just got launched into my top five. there's just so much to love here: the quaint décor, the lovely owners and, most definitely, the food. the food, the food, the food. next time i find myself in nola with time for one meal only, it's gonna be *brigtsen's* seafood platter, aka the "shell beach diet." i'm mad just thinking about it.

imbibe / devour:
gruet blanc de noir
truchard merlot
brigtsen's seafood platter
rabbit tenderloin with andouille parmesan grits cake
butternut shrimp bisque
shrimp remoulade
crawfish shortcake

café degas

french bistro

3127 esplanade avenue. corner of ponce de leon
504.945.5635 www.cafedegas.com
lunch wed - sat 11a - 2:30p brunch sun 10:30a - 3p
dinner wed - thu 6 - 10p fri - sat 6 - 10:30p sun 6 - 9p

opened in 1986. owners: jacques soulas and jerry edgar chef: ryan hughes
$$: all major credit cards accepted
brunch. lunch. dinner. full bar. reservations recommended

mid city > e05

tvh: i must admit my knowledge of french cuisine is limited. but i know good food, so therefore i felt that i could talk about *café degas*. even though it's located near the racetrack/jazz fest grounds, *café degas* feels more like provence in spring. not to sound fromage-y, but there is a clean, quiet elegance in every nook and cranny here, and even the crannies are delicious. my newly acquired accent annoyed the wait staff, but i dare you to finish a meal here and not start *parlez-vousing* yourself.

imbibe / devour:
ricard over water cocktail
sazerac cocktail
l'assiette de patés
les escargots bourguignons
la salade de chèvre tiède
mignonettes de veau au parmesan
duck & cannellini cassoulet

MESSIEURS

19

café du monde

orginal french market coffee stand
800 decatur street. corner of st. ann
504.525.4544 www.cafedumonde.com
daily 24/7 (closed christmas day)

opened in 1862
$: cash
coffee / tea. treats. first come, first served

french quarter >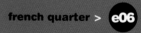

tvh: everyone who visits nola goes to *café du monde,* as they should. sitting on the mississippi river, *café du monde* is the original coffee shop. world-famous authors and dignitaries were sipping chicory-blend café au laits and eating hot beignets here a hundred years before the world-wide internet was invented. the wait staff has one mission—too keep your cup full. i like to sit here and pretend i'm surrounded by the ghosts of my favorite southern authors while they spin yarns. then people look at me like i'm nuts and i slink off to order some more beignets.

imbibe / devour:
café au lait
iced coffee
white milk
chocolate milk
orange juice
beignets
and more
beignets

café reconcile

non-profit collaborative project serving lunch and the community daily

1631 orthea castle haley boulavard. corner of terpsichore
504.568.1157 www.cafereconcile.com
mon - fri 11a - 3p

opened in 0. proprietor: craig cuccia
$: all major credit cards accepted
lunch. first come, first served

central city >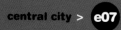

tvh: *café reconcile* is a great story. some wonderful folks in central city got together about ten years ago to mentor inner city youth, train them for work in the dining industry and teach them life skills. more than 250 graduates later, *café reconcile* is still going strong and serving absolutely delicious food. in fact, after katrina, the café was quick to get up and running again and serving good food to the good people of nola. the vibe around here, and the amazing kids, could put a smile on even the gloomiest face.

imbibe / devour:
barq's root beer
jalapeño cornbread
smothered okra
mon: red beans & rice with smoked sausage
tue: crawfish pasta
wed: pot roast
fri: shrimp creole
fried chicken everyday

casamentos

legendary oysters

4330 magazine street. corner of napoleon
504.895.9761 www.casamentosrestaurant.com
lunch wed - sun 11a - 2p dinner thu - sat 5:30 - 9p sun noon - 3p
closed jun - aug and major holidays

opened in 1919. owner / chef: t.j. casamentos
$ - $$: cash
lunch. dinner. first come, first served

uptown >

d: being a houstonite, i grew up in the middle of what i considered seafood heaven: cape cod-style fast food chains on every corner. to me, there was nothing better than a fried, triangular piece of mystery fish with a side of hush puppies and fried crunchies. after high school, my dad introduced me to oysters on the half shell—i graduated to a higher class of seafood eaters. not until i visited *casamentos* had i experienced a world class oyster bar. built in 1919, this place is a new orleans icon. if you don't do raw, no worries. the oyster loaf on pan bread is a slice of seafood heaven. arrrr, matey.

imbibe / devour:
abita amber beer
oyster loaf
trout loaf
oysters on the half shell
  (stand & eat these at the bar)
crab claws
oyster stew
fresh home-made french fries

central grocery co.

italian specialties

923 decatur street. between dumaine and st.philip
504.523.1620
tue - sat 9a - 5p

opened in 1906. owner: tommy tusa
$: all major credit cards accepted
lunch. grocery

french quarter > **e09**

tvh: i'm half sicilian, so *central grocery* in the quarter was like coming home to a place i'd only heard about from relatives long departed. i'm glad my nana aliano wasn't alive to see *central grocery or* she would have died of happiness on the spot. before this trip into yesteryear, my only muffaletta (moo-foo-let-ta) eating experience was at a chain restaurant. not good. i can now say that after eating *central grocery's* famous muffaletta, this is one of the best sandwiches i've ever eaten. i'd love to explain why, but i can't be bothered about it now, because i need to go get another.

imbibe / devour:
orleans coffee exchange coffee
home of the muffaletta
olive salad to go
stuffed artichokes
raviolis
homemade italian sausage
balocco il pandoro panettone
dry goods

clancy's

upscale neighborhood bistro
6100 annunciation street. corner of webster
504.895.1111
dinner mon - sat 5:30 - 10p

opened in 1981. owners: brad and sue hollingsworth and brian larson
chef: steve manning
$$$: all major credit cards accepted
dinner. full bar. reservations recommended

uptown > **e10**

d: *clancy's* is one of those establishments that will have you feeling as if you're living in another time and in another place. this upscale, uptown neighborhood restaurant has been serving regulars since 1981. and in that time, this place has probably seen more seersucker suits than the city has seen water. the five-star food, the elegant atmosphere and the big-hearted staff all suggest that the south shall rise again. and when the southerners rise up, they will be well fed, well mannered and dressed to kill.

imbibe / devour:
old fashioned
grilled shrimp with stone-ground bacon grits
clancy's crabmeat salad
crawfish etouffee
panee veal annunciation
filet mignon with stilton & red wine demi glaze
sweetbreads façon du chef
rissotto with lobster & mushrooms

29

cochon

cajun southern cooking

930 tchoupitoulas street. corner of south diamond
504.588.2123 www.cochonrestaurant.com
mon - fri 11a - 10p dinner sat 5:30 - 10p

opened in 2006. owners / chefs: stephen stryjewski and donald link
$$: all major credit cards accepted
lunch. dinner. full bar. reservations recommended

warehouse district > **e11**

d: my oldest sister tells a story of how i first learned to use a napkin properly. i was about twelve and she and her husband decided to take me out for a high-falutin' dinner. apparently, i was wiping food from my face with the back of my hand and then using the "napkin thingy" to clean the food from my hand. not the best way to get from point a to point b, but it worked for me. *cochon* straddles the line also. part upscale cajun, part downscale joint. part felix ungar, part oscar madison. you get the idea. where else can you wash down your rabbit and dumplings with catdaddy moonshine?

imbibe / devour:
mayhaw lemonade
bayou beer (it's got moonshine in it!)
fried boudin
smoked ham hocks with grits & gravy
rabbit & dumplings
ribs with watermelon relish
fried alligator with chili garlic aioli
lemon buttermilk pie

crabby jack's

lunch counter louisiana style
428 jefferson highway. between knox and dakin
504.833.crab
mon - sat 10:30a - 5p

opened in 2002. owner: jacques leonardi chef: paul harris
$ - $$: all major credit cards accepted
lunch. first come, first served

metairie > **e12**

tvh: some places make you feel like you're at mom's house while others make you feel like you're at your bachelor uncle's pad. welcome to *crabby jack's*, which is in the latter category based off of general vibe, not necessarily food (uncle cuisine is usually found in a bag) as this place is home to the best po'boy i've ever eaten in my life. i waddled out of *jack's* about ten pounds heavier from the grub. at my uncle's house, the same effect would have resulted from the bourbon imbibed.

imbibe / devour:
iced tea
stuffed mirilton
blackened gulffish
amazing slow-roasted duck po'boy
shrimp remoulade
homemade onion rings
side of red beans & rice

crescent city farmers market

urban farmers market

700 magazine street. 200 broadway. corner of girod
www.crescentcityfarmersmarket.org
magazine: sat 8a - noon broadway: tue 9a - 1p

opened in 1995
$: cash
market. coffee / tea. treats

downtown > **e13**

tvh: the locals make new orleans what it is. it's that simple. they come in all shapes and sizes, from the boisterous to the quiet, and they congregate in the coolest cracks and crevices of one of america's most amazing cities. one of the places where locals gather is the *crescent city farmers market*, a quintessential new orleans cornerstone. you want to sample the local goods and get a taste of what's what in this not-so-sleepy town? here it is. take your time, talk to everyone and shake a couple of hands. the stories you gather here, you might be re-telling for decades.

imbibe / devour:
smith creamery chocolate milk
angel's pralines
fresh-baked pies
beautiful fruit & veggies
handmade chocolate truffles
juicy satsumas
fresh seafood & meats

croissant d'or patisserie

a unique french breakfast experience

617 ursuline avenue. between royal and chartres
504.524.4663
wed - mon 7a - 2p

opened in 1983. owner / chef: gerard marchal
$: all major credit cards accepted
breakfast. coffee / tea. treats

french quarter > **e14**

tvh: did i hear someone say methuselah had his 80th birthday here? yep, it's true. *croissant d'or patisserie* has been open a good long time and the people of new orleans are the better for it. this dainty, beautiful place is the perfect spot to steal away to and enjoy some glorious french pastry and good coffee. i promise even if you succumb to the temptation to go out on the town and revel like it's 1999, the brioche here will tempt you to wake up early the next morning.

imbibe / devour:
good strong coffee
almond croissant
gratin potatoes & sausage
brioche
quiche
french style king cakes (during mardi gras)
strawberry napoleon
madeleines by the bag

dick & jenny's

comfort food meets high-end presentation and details

4501 tchoupitoulas street. corner of jena
504.894.9880 www.dickandjennys.com
tue - thu 5:30 - 10p fri - sat 5:30 - 10:30p

opened in 1999. owners: will and leigh peters, whiton and archana paine
chef: james leeming
$$ - $$$: all major credit cards accepted
dinner. full bar. first come, first served

uptown > **e15**

tvh: if you're anything like me, and let's hope you're not, some trips to the big easy resemble an excerpt from a hunter s. thompson novel. but even during my slightly debauched expeditions, i find it's good to breakaway and soak up a bit of sophistication (though not too much). what fits this ticket can be found along the mississippi at *dick & jenny's*. it's the perfect balance here of calm haven and comforting, yet fancy food. i can re-find my inner adult here, and that can be an important thing to connect to when you're spending time in this town.

imbibe / devour:
sazerac
94 vegaval plata, valdepenas, gran reserva
scallop ceviche, yucca chips & tuna carpacchio
beef tenderloin with mushroom risotto
dynamite napoleon, fried green tomatoes
    layered with crawfish
smoked rabbit, duck & andouille gumbo
creole cream cheese strawberry shortcake

el gato negro

authentic mexican cuisine

81 french market place. corner of barraks
504.525.9752
mon - thu 11a - 9p fri 11a - 10p sat - sun 9a - 9p

opened in 2006. owner: juan contreras chef: netzahualcoyotl contreras
$ - $$: mc. visa
breakfast. lunch. dinner. full bar. first come, first served

french quarter > **e16**

d: the word on the pot-holed street in nola is that there's a new mexican sheriff in town, and his name is *el gato negro*. being a red-blooded texican myself and a margarita connoisseur to boot, i felt the need to find out if new orleans truly had bona fide mexican fare. though over the years i've eaten about 400 po' boys in this town, until now, i don't ever recall having had an enchilada here. well, that's all changed. juan contreras is serving up his momma's central mexican recipes and he's also serving some killer margaritas. time to hoist a piñata in jackson square.

imbibe / devour:
carrot margaritas
homemade sangria
pulled pork tamales
queso fundido con chorizo dip
lamb chops guadalajara style
medallions of pork loin al casador
shrimp ceviche

elizabeth's restaurant

real food done real well

601 gallier street. corner of chartres
504.944.9272 www.elizabeths-restaurant.com
lunch wed - fri 11a - 2:30p dinner wed - sat 6 - 10p
brunch sat - sun 8a - 2:30p

opened in 1998. owner: jim harp chef: bryon peck
$$: all major credit cards accepted
brunch. lunch. dinner. full bar. first come, first served

bywater >  **e17**

tvh: i remember someone telling me *elizabeth's* had the best breakfast in town and that they had praline bacon. and i remember saying how not so delicious that sounded. then i remembered telling someone in 1983 that bill gates would never get microsoft off the ground. so obviously i'm not always the final authority on what will work. and let me tell you, the praline bacon works. so much so that i'm heading for *elizabeth's* again tomorrow morning and i'm having two orders of the praline bacon. and maybe i'll have a bloody mary for good measure.

imbibe / devour:
cajun bloody mary cocktail
praline bacon
boudin balls in creole mustard sauce
grits & grillades
big ass burger
fried chicken livers with elizabeth's pepper jelly
carolina shrimp & grits (the hangover helper)
campfire smoked rib-eye steak with hollandaise

fair grinds coffeehouse

coffee and tea community

3133 ponce de leon. between mystery and lopez
504.913.9072 www.fairgrinds.com
daily 6:30a - 10p

opened in 2002. owners: robert and elizabeth thompson
$: cash
coffee/tea. treats. first come, first served

mid city > e18

g: i have always savored the delicious conversations that my best friends and i have. you know, the type of intriguing talks where you feel like time collapses in on itself, but you leave the conversation feeling sated and stimulated. *fair grinds coffeehouse* serves this feeling in a cup. for two years now after the levees failed and water destroyed thousands of homes, *fair grinds* has supplied free coffee to the local inhabitants. i have seen many hip coffee shops, but this place is just miles beyond hip—it's got soul.

imbibe / devour:
fair trade coffees
all organic loose tea
fresh lemonade
real café au lait
yummy local-made bakery items

45

feelings cafe

romantic setting accompanied by wonderful food

2600 chartres street. corner of franklin
504.945.2222 www.feelingscafe.com
mon - thu, sun 6 - 9:30p fri - sat 6 - 10:30p sun brunch 11a - 2p
piano bar opens at 5p

opened in 1979. owners: dale de bruyne and james baird
$$ - $$$: all major credit cards accepted
brunch. dinner. full bar. first come, first served

faubourg marigny > **e19**

tvh: i have four little brothers and one little sister. i learned at a very early age not to call someone stupid no matter what he or she does, it's just mean. you'll never have to worry about someone using hurtful names at *feelings cafe*. here is where you come for a good time and truly good food that treats you well. i don't know where the name comes from, and i swear i asked, because i care. but i do know one thing. if you don't get the peanut butter pie, you're stupid.

imbibe / devour:
cafe d'aunoy coffee drink
shrimp etoufee spread
seafood baked eggplant
tournedos au poivre
veal d'aunoy
salmon mousse
peanut butter pie
french silk pie

hansen's sno-bliz

there are no shortcuts to quality
4801 tchoupitoulas street. corner of bordeaux
504.891.9788
roughly thu - sun 1 - 7p (during the hot months)

opened in 1934. owner: ashley hansen head taster: gerard hansen
$: cash
treats. first come, first served

uptown >

d: fact: the sno-ball is to new orleans as the sno-cone is to the rest of the country. fact: *hansen's sno-bliz* is the oldest known sno-ball stand in the country, opened by mary and earnest hansen in 1934. fact: ernest hansen built his patented ice-shaving machine in the '30s and it's still in operation. as ernest noted, "there is no shortcut to quality." fact: ernest and mary's granddaughter ashley now runs the shop. fact: the legendary *hansen's* is one of the greatest delights in a city chock-full of culinary wonder. come here and you'll feel twelve all over again.

imbibe / devour:
sno-bliz:
  cream of chocolate
  cream of nectar
  lava flow
  spearmint
  orangeade
  sundae

herbsaint

think locally and cook globally

701 st charles avenue. corner of girod
504.524.4114 www.herbsaint.com
lunch mon - fri 11:30a - 1:30p dinner mon - sat 5:30 - 10p

opened in 2000. owner / chef: donald link
$$$: all major credit cards accepted
lunch. dinner. full bar. reservations recommended

downtown > **e21**

tvh: i rarely use the word chic; in fact, i go out of my way not to utter the term as it reminds me of bad '80s jeans commercials. but *herbsaint* has made me re-think chic in a positive light. after all, what it really means is attractive and sophisticated, and *herbsaint* is all that. not only was i was glad that i came here, but even gladder i had the homemade pasta. and the service was so good, i was pretty sure they had mistaken me for a foreign dignitary, so i fumbled for my i.d. to prevent any ensuing international incident, and then i went back to devouring the pork belly.

imbibe / devour:
wine flights
herbsaint champagne cocktail
blood orange martini
house-made spaghetti with guanciale
seared pork belly with pickled pepper & corn risotto
herbsaint tomato & shrimp bisque
coconut cream pie with macadamia nut crust

51

iris

contemporary american cuisine

8115 jeannette street. between carrollton and dubln
504.862.5848 www.irisneworleans.com
mon - sat 6p - til close

opened in 2006. owner / chef: ian schnoebelen   co-owner: laurie casebonne
$$: all major credit cards accepted
dinner. full bar. reservations recommended

uptown > **e22**

t: *iris* is a sure sign that the south will always rise again. this homey little gem of a restaurant will restore your belief that nola is a serious food mecca. inside a charming petite house with eleven tables and a little outdoor seating area belies a serious foodie landscape of exquisitely fresh ingredients and truly masterful preparation. the minute you enter the absinthe green room with its crisp white linens and crystal fixtures, you know you're in the right place. and my goodness, *mon chere*, leave room for dessert. in nola, we live to eat and for good reason.

imbibe | devour:
a glass of pinot noir
wild striped bass
veal cheek ravioli
yellowfin tuna crusted with green peppercorn
beef short ribs
lamb osso buco
louisiana strawberries marinated with balsamic
    vinegar & black pepper with ricotta cake

jacques-imo's cafe

real n'awlins food

8324 oak street. corner of dante
504.861.0886 www.jacquesimoscafe.com
mon - thu 5:30 - 10p fri - sat 5:30 - 10:30p

opened in 1996. owner: jacques leonardi
$$ - $$$: all major credit cards accepted
dinner. full bar. reservations recommended

riverbend > **e23**

thv: if you've never heard of *jacques-imo's* and you've been to new orleans, i can only assume your layover was less than an hour long. to say this place is legendary is an understatement. jacques will likely be in residence when you venture in, and you'll see his stamp on the entire joint as this place is pure new orleans—every stereotype you've ever imagined or experienced about nola takes form here. and someday if you're lucky, you'll get to sit and eat your meal in the bed of the truck parked out front. dig into a plateful of steak and oysters, and watch the world go by.

imbibe / devour:
bloody mary
dixie beer
cajun bouillabaisse
shrimp & alligator sausage cheesecake
fried grits with shrimp & tasso sauce
country-fried venison
side of butter beans & corn maque choux
carpetbagger steak with oyster tasso hollandaise

joey k's

neighborhood restaurant

3001 magazine street. corner of seventh
504.891.0997 www.joeyksrestaurant.com
mon - fri 11a - 10p sat 8a - 10p

opened in 1989. owners: cindy and sammy farnet   chef: smitty
$ - $$: all major credit cards accepted
breakfast. lunch. dinner. full bar. coffee / tea. first come, first served

uptown > **e24**

d: *joey k's* reminds me of *cheers*, minus the boston zip code, the know-it-all mailman and the portly guy who had his very own corner barstool. so why the comparison? maybe the fact that it's a beloved local hangout with daily blackboard specials, the best all-you-can-eat catfish platter in town and a trout tchoupitoulas that'll knock your socks off. and they have the friendliest waitstaff this side of happyville. or maybe it's simply the fact that they serve ice-cold draft beer and you feel like everyone knows your name.

imbibe / devour:
abita beer
red beans & rice
shrimp magazine
trout tchoupitoulas
breaded veal
oyster & artichoke soup
fried artichoke hearts
miss cathy's brownie pie

57

la boulangerie

quintessential french bakery
4526 magazine street. between cadiz and jena
504.269.3777
mon - sat 6:30a - 5p sun 7a - 1p

opened in 1999. owner: dominique rizzo
$: cash
coffee / tea. treats

uptown >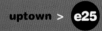

tvh: after eating at *la boulangerie*, i sincerely forgot i was in the united states. after spending a half hour or so butchering the french language with a friend over olive bread and some exquisite coffee, we left *la boulangerie* and walked out to the street. wait! why were there large cars with louisiana plates? why were there no men in berets walking the streets? okay, i was obviously a little high after indulging in my pastry-induced french fantasy, but can you blame me after gazing at the picture of the apple and puff pastry fantasy to the left? don't think so.

imbibe / devour:
coffee
almond croissant
chocolate moelleux
chocolate decadence
cream puffs
tomato fougasse
brie sandwich
delicious tartines

la crêpe nanou

french neighborhood bistro

1410 robert street. corner of prytania
504.899.2670 www.lacrepenanou.com
mon - sat 6 - 10p   fri - sat 6 - 11p

opened in 1983. owners: nanou and josie chef: son phan
$ - $$: mc. visa
dinner. full bar. first come, first served

uptown >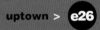

t: i have an ongoing search for the perfect french onion soup in the crescent city. though you'll find many versions around, the real deal to me is served at the oh-so-parisian spot *la crêpe nanou*, where the mussells and escargots call my name too. french chic for the budget-minded is the style of this welcoming little bistro, where the vibe of left bank paris is evoked with woven café chairs on the sidewalk and awnings that resemble metro-station architecture. i feel here like i could easily be hanging in the 6th arrondisssement.

imbibe / devour:
monmousseau brut etoile nv champagne
steamed mussels with pomme frites
crêpe au crab
crêpe antillaise
le ris de veau
café liegois
crêpe belle hélène

la petite grocery

french bistro

4238 magazine street. corner of milan
504.891.3377 www.lapetitegrocery.com
tue - thu 6 - 9:30p fri - sat 6 - 10:30p

opened in 2004. owner: joel dondis chef: justin devillier
$$$: all major credit cards accepted
dinner. full bar. reservations accepted for parties of six or more

uptown >

d: first a flower shop, then a grocery, now one of nola's finest restaurants. safe to say, *la petite grocery* won't return to peddling daisies or quarts of milk anytime soon. it's quickly garnered the attention of food critics, locals and those seeking the tastiest louisiana bouillabaisse this side of anywhere. and i must say, this place is classy—tin walls, red drapes, a polite wait staff, a cozy bar and one of the best chefs in town. wrap this all up and put it on magazine, the hippest street in town—where, if you're in need, you can also find your flowers and groceries.

imbibe / devour:
decadent wine list
steak tartare with smoked aioli & croutons
louisiana bouillabaisse
country-style pork terrine with apples & pistachios
roasted black cod
ravioli of crawfish & mascarpone
frozen sampler

63

la vita

italian eatery

3201 esplanade avenue. corner of mystery
504.948.0077 www.lavitapizza.com
lunch and dinner sun - thu 11a - midnight fri - sat 11a - 1a
brunch sat - sun 10a - 2p

opened in 2007. owner: fatma aydin
$ - $$: all major credit cards accepted
brunch. lunch. dinner. full bar. reservations accepted for parties of six or more

mid city > **e28**

tvh: ever order a meal and have it come out looking so beautiful you didn't want to cut into it with a fork? get over it. this food is gorgeous, but it deserves to be eaten, not worshipped. i'm half sicilian, so the southern italian part of me often struggles with enjoying some of the other regional italian cuisines to the fullest extent. but the good people at *la vita* have won me over. who's not a sucker for homemade lasagna and fresh-baked bread? if for some reason you think you can resist this combination, i dare you to try to resist it here.

imbibe / devour:
gnocchi
wonderful lasagna
special pizza pot pie
homemade baked breads
meat classico pizza with whole-wheat crust
venetian cannelloni
manicatta quattro formaggio
tuscan vegetable portabella

li'l dizzy's cafe

always hot and straight from the pot
1500 esplanade avenue. corner of robertson
504.569.8997
mon - fri 7a - 2:30p sat 7a - 2p

opened in 2005. owner: wayne baquet
$ - $$: all major credit cards accepted
breakfast. lunch. first come, first served

treme > e29

tvh: the baquet family are new orleans restaurant royalty. this isn't because of any blue blooded, fox hunting lineage overseas; it's because they make wonderful food, and locals have been enjoying it for generations. the environment is gentle at *li'l dizzy's*, like at a favorite relative's house. fall in love with the food, fall in love with the photos, fall in love with the surroundings; but make sure you fall in love (and eat) the bread pudding. then and only then can you meet st. peter at the gates and say you did it right while you were on earth.

imbibe / devour:
bring your own beer or wine
yummy sweet tea
shrimp omelette
trout baquet
homemade hot sausage
fried chicken
red beans & rice
bread pudding to die for

liborio

cuban restaurant

321 magazine street. corner of gravier
504.581.9680 www.liboriocuban.com
lunch mon - sat 11a - 3p dinner tue - sat 5:45 - 9p

opened in 1969. owner: felipe cortizas
$$: all major credit cards accepted
lunch. dinner. full bar. reservations accepted for parties of ten or more

downtown > **e30**

tvh: before eating at *liborio*, the only thing i knew about cuba was that their president guy wears fatigues, they drive old cars, and che guevera had an awesome merchandising contract. i definitely didn't know anything about the cuban cuisine. now i'm looking online to see if i can move there, but it looks like i can't get a flight to havana from here—so i'll just keep eating at *liborio*. i'm afraid though that i like the paella so much here, that i might get deported. hopefully i'll get sent straight to cuba.

imbibe / devour:
rum mojito
materva soda
ropa vieja
caldereta
cuban steak
seafood paella
green plantains
tres leche cake

lilette

a french italian bistro

3637 magazine street. between louisiana and napoleon
504.895.1636 www.liletterestaurant.com
lunch tue - sat 11:30p - 2p
dinner tue - thu 5:30 - 9:30p fri - sat 5:30 -10:30p

opened in 2000. owner / chef: john harris
$$$: all major credit cards accepted
lunch. dinner. full bar. reservations recommended

uptown > **e31**

d: i'm not one to take the lint brush to a pair of pants. nor am i one to iron a button-down. come to think of it, i don't own a lint brush. or an iron. i will admit, however, that when i walked into *lilette* for the first time, i felt underdressed and underpressed. there's no dress code here, but the place is just so damned sexy, you can't help but want to look good. i had no problem devouring my alaskan king crab claws even though i was in jeans, a t-shirt and chuck tailors. but i couldn't help but think the crab didn't get it's due respect.

---

imbibe / devour:
lilette rouge champagne cocktail
amaro iced tea
linstead cocktail
alaskan king crab claws (when in season)
grilled beets with goat cheese & walnuts
hanger steak with fries & marrowed bordelaise
duck confit with baby greens & vidalia onions
strawberry rhubarb tart

71

liuzza's by the track

a neighborhood joint like no other

1518 north lopez. corner of grand route st. john
504.669.3327
mon - sat 11a - 7p

opened in 1945. owner: jimmy lemarie chef: billy gruber
$ - $$: all major credit cards accepted
lunch. dinner. full bar. first come, first served

mid city > e32

tvh: i have a friend who, if he likes something tremendously, will say "that's just stupid." another example is, "winning the lottery on your birthday is just stupid." so after eating himself silly at *liuzza's*, he might say, "man, that was stupid." what i would have to say though after eating the gumbo here is "you'd be stupid not to eat the gumbo at *liuzza's*." i think our use of the word might be a bit different, but i think you get the point.

imbibe / devour:
bloody mary
po'boy's:
  bbq shrimp
  breathtaking beef
  garlic oyster
liuzza's burger
creole gumbo
shrimp remoulade

lola's

a taste of spain
3312 esplanade avenue. corner of ponce de leon
504.488.6946
daily 5:30 - 9:30p

opened in 1994. owner: angel miranda chef: lindsey mclellan
$$: cash
dinner. wine / beer only. first come, first served

mid city > e33

d: the closest i ever got to spain was dating a girl in college who was half spanish. after eating at *lola's*, i can now confidently say i've visited the country. and apparently, spain isn't on the iberian peninsula, nor is it flanked by the mediterranean. it's on esplanade and it's flanked by the mighty mississippi. *lola's* is as authentic as it gets—authentic spanish fare and sidewalk seating to boot. first, try the ajoblanco soup and then if you're not 100% certain of your whereabouts, order the paella. still not sure? get the caldereta. should you decide to run with the bulls, you'll need the energy.

imbibe / devour:
house-made sangria
seafood paella
ajoblanco soup
garlic mushrooms
caldereta stew
gazpacho soup
mussels in vinaigrette
chuflan

mandina's

creole / italian restaurant in the heart of historic new orleans

3800 canal street. corner of south cortez
504.482.9179 www.mandinasrestaurant.com
mon - thu 11a - 9:30p fri - sat 11a - 10:30p sun noon - 9p

opened in 1932. owners: cindy and tony mandina
$$: cash only
lunch. dinner. full bar. first come, first served

mid city >

tvh: in the business district, there sits a classy restaurant with a beautiful towering bar called *mandina's*. newly renovated after katrina, this quintessential new orleans restaurant is back in fine form. the mandinas run a family-friendly, fun and quirky place—but take note to get in good with the bartender as he's your ticket to a good table. and let's not forget about the food here. it is everything in the world to write home about; in fact, it deserves its own stamp.

imbibe / devour:
old-fashioned cocktail
trout meuniere
trout almandine
homemade turtle soup au sherry
crab fingers in wine sauce
shrimp cocktail
grilled shrimp over pasta bordelaise
milky way pie

mat & naddie's

in the little yellow shotgun house where freret meets the river
937 leonidas street. corner of freret
504.861.9600 www.matandnaddies.com
lunch mon - fri 11a - 2p dinner thu - sat, mon 5:30 - 9:30p

opened in 1996. owner / chef: steve schwarz
$$: all major credit cards accepted
lunch. dinner. full bar. reservations accepted for parties of two or more

uptown > **e35**

d: i don't claim to know mat and naddie. nor do i claim to know why mat's name is missing a "t." i do know that when i first went to nola with my then-girlfriend, now-wife bonnie to meet her parents for the first time, they took us to *mat & naddie's*. i remember thinking how lucky i was. lucky to have found bonnie. lucky to discover she had wonderful parents. lucky to be sitting in a quaint restaurant in the big easy, eating crispy duck leg confit and 17th ward blood orange louisiana yams. i thought about making my way down to harrah's casino that night but decided not to press my luck.

imbibe / devour:
french 75 with blood orange juice
dixie beer
wild mushroom & gruyère roulade
portobello mushroom cheesecake
grilled filet mignon with herbed compound butter
black bean barbecue shrimp
grilled yellowfin tuna medallions with catalan relish
warm spinach salad with seared johnny cake

79

mchardy's

chicken and fixin's

1458 north broad street. corner of bayou
504.949.0000
mon - sat 11a - 6:30p sun 11a - 3p

opened in 2001. owner: alvi mogilles
$: cash
lunch. dinner. first come, first served

esplanade ridge / gentilly >

tvh: i love alvi and her "white box full of love" at *mchardy's*. this box is filled with the best fried chicken i've ever eaten. if there is a food heaven (other than new orleans), alvi's been there and was sent back to teach us what good food is. the take-out-only menu here is simple. main dish: fried chicken. choice of sides: fries. i recommend the half chicken with fruit punch. recently i heard alvi filled an order for almost four thousand people at a church function. like i said, alvi's been to food heaven—so the church folk knew they were calling the right person when they placed their order.

imbibe / devour:
sweet tea
fruit punch
fried chicken
fries with a side of peppers

napoleon house

a café and bar that is the essence of new orleans

500 chartres street. corner of st. louis

504.524.9752 www.napoleonhouse.com

sun - mon 11:30a - 5p tue - wed 11:30a - 10p thu 5p - 10p fri - sat 11:30a - 11p

opened in 1936. owners: sal and maria impastato chef: sal impastato

$ - $$: all major credit cards accepted

lunch. dinner. full bar. first come, first served

tvh: in this city of food, there are many legendary places, and the family-owned since 1914, *napoleon house,* is clearly one of them. everything here is timeless from the period decoration to the classic new orleans cuisine. a legendary place must have a legendary dish—here, it's the hot muffulletta (the only hot muffuletta in town). i chased mine down with another legend—the pimm's cup. and one more legend is *napoleon house's* history. the little guy reportedly stayed here while in exile, but most folks wink when they re-tell that legend.

imbibe / devour:
the famous pimm's cocktail
sazerac cocktail
famous hot muffulettas
jambalaya
ratatouille sandwich
red beans & rice
seafood gumbo

o'delice french bakery

all manner of good things to eat and drink
6033 magazine street. corner of state
504.891.8311
mon - sat 7:30a - 6p sun 8a - 2p

opened in 2003. owner: nancy nguyen
$: mc. visa
coffee/tea. treats. first come, first served

uptown >

t: so maybe you're not the queen consort of france, but you know how to indulge as much as the next gal with a powdered wig and a mean sweet tooth. slap on the cubic zirconium encrusted tiara from your wedding, load the clan into the family truckster (instead of a horse-drawn carriage) and set forth to *o'delice* —a sugary sweet gallery of gratification. within a few short moments of surveying the wondrous landscape of assorted french pastries, pies, croissants, and other such godly items, you'll abandon your bourgeois manners to gleefully declare "let them eat cake!"

imbibe / devour:
coffee
almond butter cream cake
red velvet cake
florentines
petit fours
flourless chocolate cake
french baguettes

parkway bakery & tavern

oldest and most entertaining po' boy shop in town

538 hagan street. corner of toulouse
504.482.3047 www.parkwaypoboys.com
wed - mon 11a - 8p live music thu - sat 7 - 10p

opened in 1922. owner: jay nix
$: all major credit cards accepted
lunch. dinner. full bar. first come, first served

mid city > **e39**

g: it is such a n'awlins thing to get a po'boy from *parkway*. it's comparable to going for late night beignets at *café du monde* or a sno-ball in mid-july. here's how it works at *parkway's* po'boys. if you like roast beef, then get the roast beef. if you like shrimp, then get the shrimp. the point is that you cannot go wrong. get your sandwich, then sit down and take your time enjoying it—slowly savoring every sensuous bite of delicious po'boy goodness. just thinking about this makes me happy.

imbibe / devour:
barq's long neck root beer
po'boys:
  hot roast beef
  alligator sausage
  oyster
  golden shrimp
  hot sausage
fried hubig's pie

roman candy man

roman chewing candy
at the zoo and roaming the city
www.romancandy.com
hours vary

opened in 1915. owner: ron kottemann
$: cash
treats. first come, first served

roaming >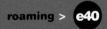

d: oh, the days of playing stickball in the street, catching fireflies and buying handmade italian taffy from a four-generations deep mule-drawn candy cart. seems like yesterday, eh? actually, it was yesterday. uptown, near st. charles. or was it downtown, off canal street? i can't recall where i last saw the *roman candy man*. he gets around, albeit slowly. if you can locate ron kottemann, his grandfather's original candy cart from 1912 and his trusty mule, patsy, slam on the brakes. the hand-pulled taffy is 75¢ a stick, and worth every tooth filling.

imbibe / devour:
taffy:
  chocolate
  vanilla
  strawberry

savvy gourmet

eats and catering, classes and cookware

4519 magazine street. corner of jena
504.895.2665 www.savvygourmet.com
lunch tue - sat 11:30a - 2:30p sun brunch 10:30a - 2:30p
store tue - sat 10a - 6p sun 10:30a - 2:30p

opened in 2005. founder: aaron m. wolfson cofounder: peter menge, jr
$ - $$: all major credit cards accepted
brunch. lunch. wine / beer. coffee / tea. catering. first come, first served

uptown > **e41**

b: what's fresh? i'll tell you what's fresh. everything at *savvy gourmet*. and i'm talking about more than just food. from the restaurant and catering service, to the hip retail store, to the slow food cooking classes, to the refined space itself. thought and preparation have gone into this culinary establishment like the makings of a fine recipe. i walked in not knowing the difference between basting and blanching and walked out ready to take on the next iron chef. plus, i had a full stomach. *chapeau outre de savvy*.

imbibe / devour:
iced mocha with smith creamery chocolate milk
watermelon lemonade
chopped crab salad with bacon, egg & tomato
croque madame with bechamel & provolone
hot meatloaf with roasted garlic mayo & arugula
learn:
cooking classes with poppy tooker

southern candymakers

the sweet spot

334 decatur street. between bienville and conti
504.523.5544 www.southerncandymakers.com
mon - sun 10a - 7p

opened in 1992. owner: peter tompkins
$: all major credit cards accepted
treats. first come, first served

french quarter >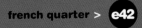

tvh: when i go to the french quarter, i never tell my doctor. well, on this trip to *southern candymakers*, i didn't tell my dentist or i would have had to say something like, "hey, dr. hime, i'm going to eat two pounds of toffees!" it just wouldn't go over so well, so i kept quiet. i was quite literally like a kid in a candy store here, except this was the tennessee williams version of willy wonka. chocoholics beware; *southern candy makers* will send you right back into rehab. but what a glorious way to go.

imbibe / devour:
melt-in-your-mouth rum chocolate,
  peanut butter or coconut pralines
double-dipped tortues (turtles)
glazed pecans
peanut brittle
white chocolate macadamia toffees
peanut pirogues
chocolate-covered marzipan

st. james cheese company

outstanding selection of artisanal and farmhouse cheeses

5004 prytania street. corner of robert
504.899.4737 www.stjamescheese.com
mon - wed 11a - 7p thu - sat 11a - 8p

opened in 2006. cheesemonger / owner: richard sutton
$ - $$: all major credit cards accepted
byob. cafe. grocery. first come, first served

uptown >

t: what do you get when a banker-turned-cheese-monger to the english royal family finds his way to uptown nola? a luscious cheese lover's paradise called *st. james cheese company*. believe me, the foods here require throwing a dinner party asap. the simplicity of this little service-oriented shop makes me dream of a bygone era of four-hour lunches in the old country. don't be afraid to sample to your heart's content as the experts here live to spread the gospel of cheese worship. even the lactose intolerant will take their chances at *st. james*.

imbibe / devour:
roquefort
english cheddar
tomme de levezu
mango pear chutney
variety of olives
fig & walnut confit
vazquez pâté
great sandwiches

sucré

a sweet boutique

3025 magazine street. corner of 7th
504.520.8311 www.shopsucre.com
sun - thu 7a - 10p fri - sat 7a - midnight

opened in 2007. owner: joel dondis   owner / pastry chef: tariq hanna
$: all major credit cards accepted
coffee / tea. treats. first come, first served

uptown >

b: i wasn't born with just one a sweet tooth, i was born with a mouth full of them. ever since i was a kid, dessert came first, then the meal. so as an adult it was no surprise to me that i fell hard for the sweet boutique called *sucré*. it's a sophisticated confectionery that caters to the inner child. you won't be disappointed. whatever your age, i can guarantee you'll leave with visions of sugarplum fairies. and if you're like me, you might need a latte to deal with the sugar hangover. when will i ever learn self control?

imbibe / devour:
haut cafe
peanut butter & jelly chocolates
lime palet
blange
lemon confit
coconut truffles
assorted macaroons
pistache griottine

surrey's cafe & juice bar

let the juices flow

1418 magazine street. between euterpe and terpsichore
504.524.3828
wed - sun 8a - 3p

opened in 2001. owner: greg surrey
$: cash
breakfast. brunch. lunch. first come, first served

lower garden district > **e45**

t: i would never have uttered the words po' boy and bananas foster in the same sentence, but there aren't any language barriers at *surrey's cafe & juice bar*. this inconspicuous and comfy place is a breakfast and brunch fave. yes sirree, i don't mean maybe. sometimes you gotta let the juices flow and sometimes you gotta feed the monkey. whatever the culinary need, you're covered with the diverse options at this low-key haunt, where they profess that every day is sunday.

imbibe / devour:
beet lemonade
shot of wheatgrass
fresh-squeezed limeade
bananas foster po' boy
boudin breakfast biscuit
huevos rancheros
black bean crab cake sandwich
costa rican breakfast

the joint

always smokin' bbq

801 poland avenue. corner of dauphine
504.949.3232 www.alwayssmokin.com
mon - tue 11:30a - 2:30p wed - sat 11:30a - 9p

opened in 2004. owners: pete and jenny breen
$ - $$: mc. visa
lunch. dinner. beer. first come, first served

bywater >

tvh: when you're hangin' outside, eating at *the joint*, you may feel like you're visiting jamaica—but don't let the smoke get in your eyes, people; you're still in bywater, and you're eating bbq. the bones here are awesome, as are pete and jenny. and if i could make some ordering suggestions, i would aim you toward a half rack of ribs and then get the: baked mac and cheese, plus a side of baked mac and cheese, and i suggest ending the meal with the baked mac and cheese. hmm-hmm good.

imbibe / devour:
sweet tea
abita beers
pulled pork sandwich
ribs, ribs & more ribs
brisket with side of slaw
sides baked beans & potato salad

verti marte

real food for real people at real prices

1201 royal street. corner of gov. nicholls
504.525.4767 www.vertimarte.com
24/7

opened in 1968. owners: sam and julie hatfield
$: all major credit cards accepted
breakfast. lunch. dinner. grocery. first come, first served

french quarter > **e47**

tvh: this being a 24-hour convenience store, my earlier, and not for publication, visits were after a night of generous libation. even then it was clear that the post-drinking eats *verti marte* made could make it past any concoction bourbon street had to offer. you walk in here and take one look at the handwritten specials on pieces of paper and get that feeling that tells you "this is going to be good." nothing fancy, but every morsel contains the basics that all the fancy food is based on. and if you need to send a postcard to tell of your adventures—grab a stamp on your way out.

imbibe / devour:
selection of imported & domestic beers
sodas to champagne
french fry po'boy
all that jazz specialty sandwich with wow sauce
shrimp philly
spinach artichoke supreme
baked macaroni
grandma's boardinghouse meatloaf

notes

eat

shop

a gallery for fine photography

rare photographs and photography books

241 chartres street. between iberville and bienville
504.568.1313 www.agallery.com
thu - mon 10:30a - 5:30p

opened in 1973. owner: joshua mann pailet
all major credit cards accepted
appraisals. portfolio review. custom framing

french quarter > **s01**

tvh: i have a problem. i can't stand to see artwork hanging crooked on a wall. i'm compelled to align the frames. so going to galleries drives me insane because i always see a slightly askew frame. at *a gallery for fine photography*, i finally got my compulsion in check so i could soak in the beauty of some of the most extraordinary photos ever taken. if you've ever dreamed of owning an original by one of the great masters of photography, this is the place to find it. don't have warren buffett's checkbook? no worries; there are prints from up-and-coming legends that will fit your budget.

covet:
original photo prints by:
  man ray
  henri cartier bresson
  diane arbus
  herman leonard
  edward west
  berenice abbott
amazing photography books

107

aidan gill for men

men's grooming and luxury shaving needs

2026 magazine street. corner of st. andrew
550 fulton street. between lafayette and poydras
504.587.9090 www.aidangillformen.com
mon - fri 10a - 6p sat 9a - 5p

opened in 1990. owner: aidan gill
all major credit cards accepted
barbershop. online shopping

lower garden district > **s02**

tvh: tucked in the lower garden district, this barber-shop to end all barbershops, *aidan gill for men*, tells a man like it is: dress well and be well groomed. real men come here, like hunter s. thompson who had one of his last shaves on site. aidan's here to teach all of us guys the lost art of being a gentleman—like how to tie a bow tie and drink whiskey (while getting a shave). and word to the wise: don't say "metrosexual" within a mile of aidan's place. really, why would you want to?

covet:
the aidan gill hot shave
aidan gill signature pre-shaving oil
truefitt & hill ultimate comfort shaving creams
mock ebony badger brush
thin-handled mock ebony razor
carrot & gibbs neckware
dashing bow ties
unique cufflinks

angelique and victoria's

high-end women's clothing, accessories and shoes

7725 maple street. between burdette and adams
504.866.1092 www.angeliqueboutiques.com
mon - sat 10a - 5:30p

opened in 1991. owner: angelique short and paula landry
all major credit cards accepted

riverbend > **s03**

t: there's a feeling that comes upon me occasionally, rising up from a well of longing that is uncontrollable. this is when i'm in the throes of a full-on clothing crave. i had this feeling as i sift through the stylish labels at *angelique and victoria's*. my head spins as i try to figure out how to purchase every single piece here. clotheshorses take heed: victoria's desirables du jour and shoes are up front and angelique's cutting-edge apparel is in residence in the back. the responsible adult in me says i have to choose only a couple of pieces. alas, the veruca salt in me whines, "i want it all now, daddy!"

covet:
l.a.m.b
see by chloe
tibi
diane von furstenburg
sigerson morrison
jimmy choo
giuseppe zanotti
the original car shoe

angelique baby

baby, kids and maternity clothing, toys and gifts

3719 magazine street. corner of amelia
504.301.2583 www.angeliquebaby.com
mon - sat 10a - 5p

opened in 2006. owner: coleen eastman and angelique short
all major credit cards accepted
online shopping. registries

uptown > s04

t: if i didn't already have a cherubic bambino to adorn and garnish, i might reproduce just so i could wheel him over to *angelique baby* and thoroughly deck him out in their plucky array of righteous kiddie clothes. thank heavens that fashions for the under-five set have finally caught up to speed. since our little angels are out there as a new-and-improved version of ourselves, they gotta represent. i also ferreted out hip retro toys, fun gift ideas for newer tots and maternity wear for the praiseworthy ladies who gave them life. ya gotta love evolution.

covet:
tea clothing
diesel kids
deux par deux
c & c t's
petit bateau undergarments
pazitos shoes
naturino shoes
bella materna maternity line

113

as you like it silver shop

flatware, holloware and jewelry

3033 magazine street. corner of 8th
504.897.6915 www.asyoulikeitsilvershop.com
mon-fri 11a - 5p sat 10a - 5p closed mon during the summer

opened in 1972. owner: duncan cox
all major credit cards accepted
online shopping. registries

uptown > **s05**

t: calling captain jack sparrow… or anyone else looking for a pirate's treasure trove of silver. *as you like it* is the place to hit the jackpot, with no digging required. in fact, they'll do the digging for you with their search service "wishlist" for discontinued and hard-to-find american tea services, trays and flatware for those with dwindling collections. there is a veritable bounty of victorian pieces, art nouveau to art deco, gilt-cloisonne eggs in the style of faberge, and even tiffany teething rings for *le bebe*! blackbeard must be spinning at the thought of all this treasure.

covet:
gorham flatware
reed & barton flatware
silver baby rattles
vintage russian demitasse spoon set
beautiful cuff links & earrings
whiting division egyptian soup ladles
5pc vintage condiment set

bamboo apothecary

high-end apothecary and spa

4112 magazine street. corner of marengo
504.895.1664 www.bambooapothecary.com
mon - sat 10a - 6p

opened in 2006. owner: jill painter
all major credit cards accepted
online shopping. spa services. custom orders / design

uptown > s06

t: when you think of the word apothecary, it conjures images of white labcoats, medieval utensils and archaic elixirs. in the modern world, there's a little haven uptown called *bamboo apothecary*, which loosely translates to "pharmacy of zen beauty." you won't find unnamed jars of alchemy here, but you will discover a rare place of heightened beauty refinement. and remember that the bamboo plant is a symbol for luck and longevity. coincidence? i don't know about you, but i'll take all the help i can get.

covet:
la mer body lotion
bond no.9 perfume
susan posnik cosmetics
soothing manicures & pedicures
ray simons age-erasing facial oil
red flower skin care products & spa treatments
natura bisse skin care products & signature facial

belladonna

retail therapy and day spa
2900 magazine street. corner of 6th
504.891.4393 www.belladonnadayspa.com
tue, fri - sat 9a - 6p wed-thu 9a - 8p

opened in 1989. owner: kim dudek
all major credit cards accepted
registries. gift baskets

uptown > **s07**

t: do you ever forget to just "be"? are you a mover and shaker in need of an existential makeover and body-mind renewal? i thought so. well, these days you must make an appointment with yourself for personal restoration and wellness. for my restoral i chose *belladonna*. within a three-hour time span i was detoxed, uplifted, soothed, waxed and purified. if you wanna share your "be" time with your honey, go for the "be together" spa rendezvous. and after you are revived, do some re-stocking of gifts for self and friends. remember, all you have is this moment.

covet:
any of the "be" spa services
french bride plates & platters
lafco house & home candles
graphic image metallic clutches
lazy dog cookie co. dog treats
hable construction totes
sai kai bowls
mor marshmallow sugar crystal body scrub

bellanoche

bedding and sleepware

3632 magazine street. corner of antonine
504.891.6483 www.belladonnadayspa.com/bellanoche1.html
mon - sat 10a - 6p

opened in 2001. owner: kim dudek
all major credit cards accepted
registries. custom orders. design services

uptown >  s08

t: a beautiful night is exactly what i had after luxuriating in the deliciously soft and sumptuous linens i scored at *bellanoche*. in a perfect world, one would have oneself thoroughly serviced at super spa *belladonna* and then pop over to visit its sister store for new bedding and pj's to round out a day of pure self indulgence and pleasure-seeking gratification. there'll be no need for sheep-counting, white noise machines, or heavy pharmaceuticals after shopping here. nighty-night!

covet:
bella notte bedding
pine cone hill bedding
kumi kookoon loungewear
prairie chic laundry detergent
andrew morgan throws
provincial-style quilts
kaffe fassett for dash & albert area rugs
home fragrances

bottom of the barrel antiques

this ain't your grandma's antique shop

1209 decatur street. corner of governor nicholls
504.202.8577 www.bottomofthebarrelantiques.com
mon - sun noon - 10p

opened in 2005. owners: greg rackham and sandra callahan
cash

tvh: *bottom of the barrel antiques* is a bit of a misnomer as there's nothing "bottom" about this place except for maybe their prices which are pretty darn low. if i ever wanted to try to recreate the '50s black pleather bar with stools (it also had white flamingos on it) that was at my grandpa's house, i would come here first to search. there's a lot of exceedingly cool stuff here and many, many items that were around well before my grandpa's pleather bar was a glimmer in his eye.

covet:
full bar from the '40s
beautiful chandeliers
victorian armoires
salvaged stained glass
vintage iron gates
amazing rugs

123

dominique giordano

jewelry design

5420 magazine street. corner of jefferson
504.895.3909 www.dgiordana.com
mon - sat 10a - 5p

opened in 2000. owner: dominique giordano
all major credit cards accepted
online shopping

uptown >

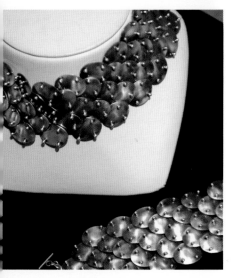

t: jewelry is no longer something to wear only to complete a look. *dominique giordano* makes jewelry that becomes a part of the wearer and therefore transcends the clothing worn. her clever and original designs can be worn with everything from a daytime linen pantsuit to an evening black strapless extravaganza. in fact, dominque's caviar ring looked pretty darn good with my nightgown. in the long run, i think the goal of purchasing jewelry, as with art, is this: when adding to what should be a very personal collection, pieces should reflect your evolution as a person.

covet:
feather coral collection
fan earrings
feather chain patina bracelet
bloom necklace
forged rings
teardrop earrings
lotus bloom lariat

eclectic home

timeless interiors and unique gifts

8133 oak street. between carrollton and durbin
504.866.6654 www.eclectichome.net
mon - fri 10a - 5:30p sat 10a - 5p

opened in 2000. owner: penny francis
all major credit cards accepted
custom orders / design

uptown > **s11**

tvh: i have renamed *eclectic home* "this is what my house will never look like." well, of course, unless i hire the team here to decorate. if you've ever fantasized that your home would be like the perfect homes in magazines where folks walk around wearing wonderful clothing, sipping champagne and listening to classical music, you'll want to stop by and absorb what doesn't need to be a fantasy. just make some reality adjustments, and you'll find everything you might need to create your dream home right here.

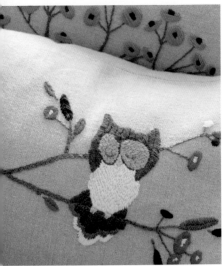

covet:
metal cast coral lamp
casablanca lamp
samusta vase
metal vases
guilded songbird paintings
iron wall art
chinoiserie wine holder
resin mirrors

127

fleur de paris

custom millinery, contemporary and couture clothing

523 royal street. corner of pirates alley
504.525.1899 www.fleurdeparis.net
mon - sun 10a - 6p

opened in 1980. owner: joseph parrino
all major credit cards accepted
custom orders

french quarter > **s12**

t: there's a wonderful sort of time warp on royal street in the heart of the french quarter. this is where you'll find *fleur de paris*, a remarkable shop that seems to be part paris in the '30s and part true southern grace back in the gentler days. all i could think of was how great it would be to show up at the kentucky derby wearing one of their sublime creations. i can see myself now standing tall in the winner's circle, mint julep in hand and work of art on my head. i shall be the envy of all.

covet:
custom millinery
derby hats
vintage veiling
over 1,000 handcrafted hats
feathers, buckles & buttons
couture dresses
katharine baumann crystal purses
garter belts

hazelnut

fine gifts and home accessories
5515 magazine street. between joseph and octavia
504.891.2424 www.hazelnutneworleans.com
mon - sat 10a - 6p

opened in 2003. owners: tom cianfichi and bryan batt
all major credit cards accepted
online shopping. registries

uptown > s13

t: "toile meets 21st century" is a fitting design descriptor for this cool little uptown find. at *hazelnut*, you could literally find 99% of your decorative add-ons to pull off a whole new interior look. mix and match is the name of the game here as you'll find asian-inspired jonathan adler vases right next to gilded byzantine glassware with a french iron candelabra as an accent. take *hazelnut's* cue, and take home a few eclectic pieces from here to mix with your tasteful furniture. all your friends will think you've got some serious interior design chops.

covet:
exclusive new orleans toile
blue bird etched glasses
mother of pearl salad servers
pewtered louisiana letter openers
urchin bowls
alison evans coastal ceramics
laurel wilder art glass
ray barloga prints

house of lounge

live, life, love lingerie

2044 magazine street. corner of josephine
504.671.8300 www.houseoflounge.com
mon - sat 11a - 6p sun noon - 5p

opened in 1998. owner: edith leblanc
all major credit cards accepted

lower garden district > **s14**

b: i'm in the mood for some new lingerie. for that matter, when is a woman not in the mood for loungewear that makes her feel irresistable? maybe only when feeling exceedingly grumpy. but most of the time, undergarments are a coveted accessory, and *house of lounge* caters to ladies' wildest fantasies (and maybe to the special someones in their lives). from the sexy corsets to the playful cami sets, the lacy bras to the "little somethings," the ladies of this house will no doubt get you in the mood for looking and feeling super fine.

covet:
madame undergarments
felina scarlet unlined bra
la perla lingerie
beautiful cami sets
kimonos
derek rose handkerchiefs
hanky panky panties
jimmy jane layerable essential fragrances

hové

old-world new orleans parfumeur

824 royal street. between st. ann and dumaine
504.525.7827 www.hoveparfumeur.com
mon - sat 10a - 5p

opened in 1931. owner: amy d. van calsem wendel
all major credit cards accepted
gift baskets. custom orders

french quarter > s15

t: it is approximated that the human nose has one thousand different sensors. our primitive sense of smell can more strongly trigger memory than any other sense. this is probably why, upon entering this lovely scent-filled maison, i was transported to my past life as a corseted, apple-cheeked aristocrat perched at a louis the fourteenth vanity in provence, spotting drops of rosewater behind my ears. lovingly established in 1931, *hové* is a family-run parfumerie that has been helping new orleanians smell like royalty for four generations.

covet:
hové:
 spanish moss luxury fragrance
 man trap luxury fragrance
 tea olive french-milled perfumed soap
 gardenia room spray
 men's & women's scented oils
 bubble bath & shower gels
 handmade powder puffs

idea factory

american woodcraft heirloom toys for kids of all ages

838 chartres. corner of dumaine
504.524.5195 www.ideafactoryneworleans.com
mon - sat 10a - 6p sun 10a - 5p

opened in 1974. owner: kenny ford
all major credit cards accepted
online shopping. custom orders

french quarter > s16

tvh: wood. who knew so many wonderful things could be made from this substance? okay, maybe the dutch knew. but so did the man who started the *idea factory*. name an object or a game to enjoy, even an instrument, and it's here made out of wood. the french quarter has so many delights, it's nearly impossible to explain some of them; but i can easily describe to you the glorious smell of the wood shop where "wood graphics" are made. the *idea factory* is something too magical to behold; in fact, it almost takes the word unhappiness out of your vocabulary.

covet:
dreidels
whirligigs & tops
circus trains
chess sets & other mind games
made by me toy kits
beautiful puzzles
handmade wood graphics
brian kidwell junk sculpture

la belle nouvelle orleans antiques

antiques and architectural accents
2112 magazine street. corner of jackson
504.581.3733 www.labellenouvelleorleans.com
mon - sat 10a - 5p

opened in 2002. owners: fernando promoslovsky and natalia skef
all major credit cards accepted

lower garden district > s17

d: if a guy wants to furnish his house with antique treasures and architectural accents from argentina, france, italy, spain, england and numerous other countries that i've never been to, he'd best go see fernando and natalia at *la belle nouvelle orleans*. the antiques and artifacts they've gathered here remind me of my grandparents' house. or, what my grandparents house would have looked like if they'd been world-traveling, antiques-loving folks with degrees in treasure hunting and architectural wizardry.

covet:

argentinian, french, italian & spanish
   architectural treasures
vintage ironwork gates & doors
grafonola record player
victor talking machine
painted tiles from england
beautiful vintage wall sconces
cast-iron fluted columns

le garage

pieces from the past and present
1234 decatur street. between governor nicholls and barracks
504.522.6639
daily noon - 6p

opened in 1984. owner: marcus fraser
all major credit cards accepted

french quarter > **s18**

tvh: if liberace, my great-grandmother, hunter s. thompson (yeah, i know—second mention of the man), john waters, roger corman and andy warhol all spent three weeks together on a desert island doing peyote and watching '50s musicals then came to the quarter via singapore, barcelona, amsterdam (an extended stay here, if you know what i mean) and london picking up antiques and oddities along the way, you'd have *le garage*. in my mind, this glorious jumble makes owner marcus's cool factor an eleven.

covet:
vintage mardi gras crew costumes
vintage porcelain serving dishes
ornate tea cup set
retro hot pants
porcelain poodle dog
everything and anything you can
  imagine and then some

lemieux galleries

arts, crafts and framing

332 julia street. corner of commerce
504.522.5988 www.lemieuxgalleries.com
mon 11a - 5p tue - sat 10a - 6p

opened in 1983. owner: denise berthiaume
all major credit cards accepted

di: in the heart of the art district on julia street stands *lemieux galleries*. as i stepped through the welcoming glass door, the thought rushed through my head that this was a glimpse into the artistic soul of new orleans. and what a powerful, color-jammed, edgy soul this city has. suddenly i wanted to dance to a little jazz and muse "yo right" while i bobbed my head. the bursting creativity in this place screamed for an appearance of the saint… or maybe just the sinner… that rattled in my soul.

covet:
ben t. shamback plastic bag
alan gerson's oil on board paintings
pat benard bather's ceramic piece
mary lee eggart colored pencil &
  watercolor pieces
luz maria lopez's mixed media on burlap
margo manning jewelry

louisiana loom works

distinctive hand-woven products

616 chartres street. corner of wilkinson
504.566.7788 www.customragrugs.com
fri - wed 11a - 7p

opened in 1997. owners: walt and ronda rose
all major credit cards accepted
custom orders

french quarter > **s20**

tvh: luckily i had a girlfriend in college who owned a loom. well hold on. maybe not luckily when i think of it in the grand scheme of things. but years down the line, i can now at least think of a loom without seeing it as a torture device. in fact, the new mature me can see that looms create beautiful things, like rag rugs. *louisiana loom works* in the quarter can and will make you a custom-crafted rag rug out of durable cotton in whatever color or colors you wish. whereas my old girlfriend could only make me crazy.

covet:
custom-made rag rugs in sizes:
  2 1/2′ x 5′
  4′ x 6′
  5′ x 8′
  8′ x 10′
  10′ x 12′
  (or any size you want just about!)

louisiana music factory

cajun, blues, jazz, zydeco : the music that moves you

210 decatur street. corner of iberville
504.586.1094 www.louisianamusicfactory.com
mon - sat 10a - 7p sun noon - 6p

opened in 1991. owner: barry smith
all major credit cards accepted
online shopping

french quarter > s21

LOUISIANA BLUES

Professor Longhair

tvh: i saw an in-store performance here in 2004 and it knocked my socks off. you know how every town has that one record store that really gets their finger on the pulse of the city? there's *waterloo* in austin and *homer's* in omaha. in nola it's this place, the *louisiana music factory*. right in the middle of everything, you'd think it might be overly touristy here, but it's not. dive into the stacks while talking to the clerks and learning about leroy jones and the people who drive jazz, dixieland and the heartbeat of this remarkable city. i feel the ghost of satchmo brush by.

covet:
lp's, dvd's & cd's:
    professor longhair
    rebirth brass band
    bally who
    alvin batiste
    buckwheat zydeco
    boo zoo chavis
    marcia ball

lux

salon and products

3141 ponce de leon. between mystery and lopez
504.301.2953 www.lux-salonblends.com
tue - sat 11a - 6p by appt. sun and mon

opened in 2006. owner: erin peacock
all major credit cards accepted
gift baskets

mid city > **s22**

b: there i was, ready to wear my brand-new sandals when i realized i was in desperate need of a pedicure. ugg... whether it's a pedicure, a manicure, or a massage you are in search of, *lux* has what you want. erin and her staff are ready to craft their services to meet your individual needs and cater to those desperate moments. sit back and relax because the toughest decision you'll need to make will be on whether to go with coney island cotton candy pink or cha-ching cherry red for your toes although you could tax yourself and do a bit of shopping while the varnish is drying.

covet:
all products sold are made by companies in new orleans:
  agera recovery cream
  agera ultralucent sunscreen
  akeewakee products
  queen b soaps
  alexia pulitzer stationary
  pink grapefruit & cassia candles

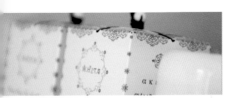

meilleur joaillerie

estate, contemporary and eclectic costume jewelry

516 royal street. corner of st. louis
504.525.9815
mon - sun 10a - 6p

opened in 1980. owner: linda laudumiey
all major credit cards accepted

french quarter > **s23**

b: my grandmother had a strict rule: no grandchildren were allowed upstairs in her house. but because we were curious kids, we would sneak upstairs to snoop. *meilleur joaillerie* reminds me of my grannylou's boudoir which was beautifully decorated with toile wallpaper, a chandelier hanging over the vanity and jewelry boxes overflowing with gorgeous pieces. she was a very stylish southern lady, and i've always wanted to emulate her and her luscious boudoir. after discovering *meilleur joaillerie*, now i can. it will be nice not to have to sneak around to play dress-up.

covet:
parisian-influenced, custom-designed
  charm necklaces
charming vintage jewelry boxes
gorgeous estate jewelry
beautiful & well-priced chandeliers
antique brooches
'30s platinum french art deco circle rings

n.o. surf shop

surfboards, apparel and sandals

6116 magazine street. corner of henry clay
504.891.1616 www.nosurfshop.com
mon - sat 10a - 5:30p

opened in 2004. owners: mary carol chenet and rob owen
all major credit cards accepted

uptown > **s24**

tvh: my friend woody taught me how to surf a couple years ago in san diego. that's san diego, california. where there's an ocean. never did it occur to me that there's surf everywhere, even on the southern louisiana coast. dude, was i narrow-minded. thank goodness the folks at the *n.o. surf shop* have been keeping the stoke alive. i had to keep reminding myself i wasn't in hawaii or la jolla when i was here as they have everything the cajun surfer needs. son of a gun, i'll hang big ten, on the bayou.

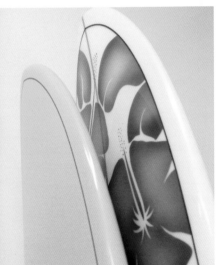

covet:
carver boards
gravity boards
rainbow flip-flops
custom designed t's
von zipper glasses
billabong apparel
board rental

153

neophobia

retro furnishings and décor

2855 magazine street. corner of sixth
504.899.2444 www.neophobia-nola.com
daily 11a - 6p

opened in 2006. owners: vic loisel and amanda frank
all major credit cards accepted
online shopping

uptown > **s25**

d: sometimes when you think you've found something, it turns out that it's something totally different. case in point, *neophobia* on magazine street. at first sight i was pretty sure it was a neon beer sign shop. apparently, i was wrong and fortunately for all those people who don't need or want a beer sign, i found something cooler: the best retro store this city has to offer. *neophobia* is loaded with mod furnishings, décor and clothing mostly from the '50s to the '70s. and though i didn't leave with any neon, i did score a george nelson clock and an old skateboard. sweet.

covet:
vintage george nelson clock
'60s ernestine of solerno fruit plates
mod '60s orange lamps
beautiful italian wall tiles
vintage skateboards
amazing floor lamps
vintage bamboo framed mirror

155

new orleans artworks
at new orleans glassworks & printmaking studio

on-site glass blowing, gallery and so much more

727 magazine street. between notre dame and girod
504.529.7277 www.neworleansglassworks.com
summer hours mon - fri 10:30a - 5:30p winter hours mon - sat 10:30a - 5:30p

opened in 1990. proprietor: geriod baronne
all major credit cards accepted
classes. commissions. repairs

warehouse district > **s26**

tvh: *edward scissorhands* was a strange and fascinating tale about an odd creature who could carve mystical objects out of just about anything with his, well, scissor hands. probably the same reason i was fascinated by this movie, is why i'm intrigued by what's going on at *new orleans artworks.* this is creativity heaven, with folks learning about and creating everything from glass, jewelry and print making to metal sculpture. damn, there are cool pieces all over this place, and the true magic is that they are being made by people just like you and me.

covet:
rondell sculpture
relationship piece
pyrex bracelets
blown-glass chandeliers
creative metal work
art sugar blowing & chocolate sculpture
  (during the august art event: white linen nights)

pied nu

trendsetting boutique

5521 magazine street. corner of octavia
504.899.4118 www.piednuneworleans.com
mon - sat 10a - 5p

opened in 1995. owners: sallee boyce and priscilla o'quinn
all major credit cards accepted
online shopping. custom orders

uptown >

t: i once had an idea that i would open a fancy ladies' store called "the best of everything," a discriminatingly edited one-stop shop to find the best of whatever you're looking for to adorn your world, whether it be yourself or your surroundings. well, *pied nu* beat me to it. you walk in here and it's perfection. there's everything from chic furniture to smart clothing, gorgeous jewelry to a bevy of beauty booty. even though they brought to life my "idea" first, i could not have done it any better. well done, *pied nu*.

covet:
dosa slip dresses
sari gueron clothing
cathy waterman jewelry
anthony nak jewelry
john derian decoupage
pee wee cocktail table
brickhouse scented lip balm
burn liquid body lotion

quarter past time

vintage watches and collectibles

606 chartres street. corner of toulouse
504.410.0010
daily (closed wed) 6a - 6p

opened in 1998. owner: julio canosa
all major credit cards accepted

french quarter > **s28**

tvh: my buddy hugh is a watch connoisseur. he can tell you what brand and year a timepiece is from a hundred yards away. this is an impressive skill, though along with this ability, he likes to check the time constantly, so he's a bit annoying to watch movies with. i may not know as much about watches (and am not obsessed with telling time), but i enjoy slipping into a *quarter past time* and looking at the vintage watches, of which there's a bounty here. there's something regal about these timepieces, and believe me, strapping on a 1930 vacheron constantin could make anyone feel regal.

covet:
vintage watches:
  rolex
  iwc
  patek philippe
  vacheron
beautiful howard pocket watch
unique cufflinks
vintage emerson radio

ropa fashion loft

contemporary women's clothing

4228 magazine street. between general pershing and milan

504.309.9772 www.myspace.com/ropafashionloft

mon - fri 11a - 6p sat 11a - 6p

opened in 2007. owners: patricia gattuso and krystal manzanares

all major credit cards accepted

uptown > **s29**

b: clean lines, bold color, interesting textures. you might think i'm talking about architecture but i'm not... i'm talking about fashion, to be exact, the clothing at *ropa fashion loft*. i've always been a fan of modern buildings and design and the elements that make them compelling, so there's no wondering why i'm drawn to the contemporary clothing at this uptown boutique. maybe when i'm wearing my new rebecca beeson dress, i'll just pose strategically by some of my favorite buildings for the ultimate juxta-position of style.

covet:
kasil jeans
level 99 jeans
rebecca beeson
ropa private label candles
lulu via tunic dresses
jully kang babydoll dresses
chinese laundry shoes

scriptura

essential paper for artful living

5423 magazine street. between octavia and jefferson
504.897.1555 www.scriptura.com
mon - sat 11a - 5p

opened in 1997. owner: sallie jones
all major credit cards accepted
custom orders

uptown > **s30**

t: my husband won my heart with a few haiku he jotted onto construction paper with accompanying watercolors and sent via the u.s. post. so i have a soft spot for all kinds of correspondence—letters, announcements, invitations... anything. i think it's truly a lost art in this harried, hi-tech age. with an elegant new orleans style, *scriptura* is in the business of artful correspondence. you'll soon be coming up with reasons to send out announcements for anything under the sun and searching for some pen pals, just so you can visit *scriptura* often.

covet:
peculiar pair press
page stationery
glass pens
wax seals
fine italian leather journals
handmade wrapping papers

serendipitous masks

the place for wondrous things

831 decatur street. corner of madison
504.522.9158 www.serendipitousmasks.com
thu - mon 10a - 6p

opened in 1967. proprietors: don fraser and m. hessler
all major credit cards accepted
custom orders / design

french quarter > **s31**

tvh: more than likely someone you know has been to mardi gras in new orleans and has slept on a curb after four straight days of treachery. but as the locals know, this debauchery is not what the city or the celebration is all about (for the most part). one of the best things about mardi gras is on fat tuesday when everybody is jamming the streets, wearing masks and throwing caution to the wind. to find the other face that's right for you, head to the city's best mask store—*serendipitous masks*. here you can find your alter ego, or hey, maybe just the new you.

covet:
masks:
  custom carnival designs
  metal laser cut
  local handmade leather
  beautiful italian carnival
carnival scepters
crowns & tiaras
beaded headdresses

shoefty

women's and men's shoes, clothes and accessories

6010 magazine street. corner of state
504.896.8737 www.shopshoefty.com
mon - sat 10a - 6p

opened in 2002. owner: sarah winston
all major credit cards accepted
online shopping. registries

uptown > **s32**

d: i'll admit it. i'm a guy and i have a shoe fetish. i've had it since fifth grade. first sign of my troubles came when i traded jeff gray an "air supply" cassette tape for his gently-worn pair of checkered vans. things haven't changed much since then, except that i now have a closet devoted to shoes. thanks to *shoefty*, i may now have to knock out a wall and add on. i left here with two pairs: the vans schwinn stingray slip-ons and the martin margiela canvas ankle boots. this place was so right up my alley that i also shopped for my wife's birthday and valentine's day both. hel-lo, one-stop shop!

covet:
shoes:
  laurence dacade
  martin margiela
  loeffler randall flats
clothing:
  mayle
  rachel comey
  phillip lim 3.1

southern fossil & mineral exchange

natural history gallery and shop

2049 magazine street. between josephine and st. andrew
504.523.5525 www.southernfossil.com
mon - sun 10:30a - 5p

opened in 1997. owner: robert mcdade
all major credit cards accepted

lower garden district > s33

tvh: *southern fossil & mineral exchange* is a must visit if you're looking for an off-beat shopping experience. cloaked in plain sight amid the lower garden district, this gem (ahem) houses the carcasses of a number of formerly living things. you'll be hard-pressed to make it through this shop without whistling the "indiana jones" theme song. though i don't have the time to travel the world, i felt pretty caught up on its wildlife after a visit here. oh, and before you fret about how to get that six-foot stuffed rattlesnake onto the plane, the kind folks here provide shipping everywhere.

covet:
shadow-boxed butterflies
shadow-boxed dung beetle
fossil stoneware
amethyst cathedrals
jackrabbit skeleton
beautiful minerals
taxidermic rattlers
alligator museum opening next door soon!

spring

modern women's clothing

5525 magazine street. corner of octavia
504.896.9185
mon - fri 10a - 6p sat 10a - 5p

opened in 1999. owner: bethany oubre
all major credit cards accepted

uptown > s34

b: i'm an "i wish" girl when it comes to traveling. "i wish" i'd brought my navy flats. "i wish" i'd brought my cashmere wrap. "i wish" i'd brought my evening clutch. i'm always wishing for that something that is missing from my suitcase. well, hallelujah! thank goodness there's a boutique like *spring*. no matter what the season, it's a great place to pick up that little something you left behind. from designer threads to casual t's to the much-needed accessory, *spring* has you covered. just be careful, ladies. you could find yourself wishing for an extra piece of luggage.

covet:
three dots
trina turk
calvin klein
525 america
hobo handbags
abs evening wear

style lab

exclusive store for men
3641 magazine street. corner of antonine
504.304.5072 www.stylelabformen.com
mon - fri 11:30a - 6p sat 10:30a - 5p

opened in 2004. owners: cristy mcnabb and jennifer webber
all major credit cards accepted

uptown > **s35**

d: i'm a sucker for vintage motorcycles. i've occasionally threatened my wife with the idea of owning a bike with a sidecar attachment, to which she has repeatedly said, "never." so why all the bike talk? because the *style lab* has strategically placed a royal enfield motorcycle on their front lawn—just the thing to lure a fella like myself inside. here you can find the biggest names in men's fashion, from ben sherman to paul smith, modern amusement to penguin. these are the kind of duds that should never be concealed inside a four-dour, hard-top sedan.

covet:
ted baker
modern amusement
trovata
paul smith
john varvatos
g-star
7-diamonds
jack spade

sweet pea & tulip boutique

women's clothing, shoes and accessories

618 chartres street. between nashville and magazine
(see website for other locations)
504.899.4044   www.sweetpeatulip.com
mon - sat 10a - 6p sun 11a - 5p

opened in 2002. owners: bom and mignon perrotta
all major credit cards accepted

uptown > **s36**

b: i'm sure you've heard the expression "you look like a million bucks." well, if you shop at *sweet pea & tulip,* you get the look without spending the loot. the sweet pea-oples at this uptown boutique will guide you through a mix of the latest contemporary trends and retro throwbacks, giving you the options you desire at a deal no less. from cool frocks to designer denim, *sweet pea & tulip* is one-stop shopping at its finest. so go ahead, dress like a million bucks. but keep most of your dollars in the bank where they belong.

covet:
super lucky cat
free people
voom
great assortment of denim
interlud dresses
yumi kim

swirl

sensational wines

3143 ponce de leon street. between mystery and lopez
504.304.0635 www.swirlinthecity.com
mon - fri 11a - 8p sat 11a - 7p

opened in 2006. owners: beth ribblett and kerry tully
all major credit cards accepted
gift baskets. bi-weekly wine tastings. classes

mid city > **s37**

g: i frequent *swirl* often, and with good reason. the place is stocked with excellent wines at fair prices and the staff is so ridiculously knowledgeable—they can pair wine with anything. if you think you have your mind made up about a wine, then i guarantee they can change your mind. on my last visit to *swirl*, i was treated to a taste of a funky blue cheese, and i mean funky—it was maybe a bit too much for my amateur palette. then i tasted a sweet dessert wine afterward and the whole experience was transformed. my tastbuds were wholly entertained.

covet:
brancaia ilatraia italian wine
duval-leroy brut champagne
enzo boglietti dolcetto d'alba
orin swift cellars, the prisoner, zin blend
tegernseerhof, gruner veltiner
bastianich vespa bianco
all the chilean & argentinian wines… yum!
friday free for all

the kite shop jackson square

kites for young and old

542 st. peter street. on jackson square
504.524.0028 www.kiteshopneworleans.com
daily 10a - 6p

opened in 1972. owner: sally fontana
all major credit cards accepted

french quarter > **s38**

tvh: there are so many memories to enjoy from childhood, especially if you had the great fortune of being raised in my family. a kite is just the thing to trigger these memories. walking into *the kite shop*, especially after already having your mind opened up by jackson square, gives you that sense of wonder we often lose as adults. smiles abound on both young and old faces. it's incredible that something as simple as brightly colored fabric that's constructed to fly, could bring such glee. though looking at the instructions on how to build some of these could make me cry.

covet:
stunt kites:
  prism nexus
  revolution
beautiful wind socks
kid's toys
mardi gras flags
people puppets

the sword and pen
formerly le petit soldiershop

the historic french quarter's little history shop

528 royal street. corner of st. louis
504.523.7741
mon - sun 10a - 5:30p

opened in 1965. owner: scott condello
all major credit cards accepted

french quarter > **s39**

tvh: if it's been shot, shot at or worn while shooting, you can find it here at *the sword and pen* (formerly *le petite soldier shop*). civil war buffs beware—you are liable to spend a week in this place and if you're like me, a lot of money. i felt as though it was thirty years ago and mom had dropped me off at the carnival with no adult supervision and a debit card. after leaving i felt like i needed to call napoleon and tell him not to fight a land war in russia in the wintertime. but alas, i simply took my bounty and went off to set up miniature soldiers on a bar and recreate the battles myself.

covet:
british royal navy officer's hat
pre civil war perfume bottle
confederate swords
coin collection
envelopes from the civil war sent to soldiers
hand painted civil war soldiers

uptown costume and dancewear

dress up your life

4326 magazine street. corner of napoleon
504.895.7969 www.myspace.com/uptowncostume
tue - fri noon - 6p sat 10a - 5p hours vary based on season

opened in 1988. owner: cheryl berlier
visa

uptown >

b: how often do you have the chance to be president nixon, the queen of sheba or elvira, mistress of the dark? probably not too often. well, if you dig dressing up—and this is probably the best town in the continental united states to do it in—*uptown costume and dancewear* will be able to outfit your wildest desires. i think we all wish we could be someone else from time to time and why not? life's short. so if next week you decide you want to dress up like the queen of england, well then, hail to the queen.

covet:
costumes!
danskin & capezio dancewear
theatrical make-up
wigs & feather boas
costume jewels
majorette boots
batons

w.i.n.o. (wine institute new orleans)

wine school · wine tasting room · wine store

610 tchoupitoulas. corner of lafayette
504.324.8000 www.winoschool.com
mon - thu noon - 9p fri - sat noon - 10p

opened in 2007. owners: bryan burkey and leslie castay
all major credit cards accepted
classes. professional certification. 10% case discounts. custom orders

warehouse district > **s41**

tvh: i love newfangled gadgetry. the only thing i know less about than digital whiz-bangs is wine. luckily that's why there's *w.i.n.o.*—what you don't know about wine, they'll teach you. i was just as impressed with their knowledge as they were with my lack. not only do they have a comprehensive class schedule, but they also have a very fancy machine that uses an official *w.i.n.o.* refillable tasting card. you put it into a slot, then the gizmo pours you a taste of your choosing. and no worries, the pros won't judge your selection; they're just happy you're trying.

covet:
wines from all over the world
  for tasting and buying
classes:
  intro to wine
  pinot envy
  monster wines
an assortment of cheeses & small plates
  to accompany your tasting

yvonne la fleur

european shopping in the heart of the big easy

8131 hampson street. corner of south carrollton
504.866.9666 www.yvonnelafleur.com
mon - sat 10a - 6p thurs 10a - 8p

opened in 1969. owner: yvonne la fleur
all major credit cards accepted
registries. gift baskets. custom orders

riverbend >

di: *yvonne la fleur* manages to straddle the line between two worlds and eras. the one world is the fictionalized one of anne rice's new orleans. it feels like yvonne could have been the milliner and dressmaker for the era of lestat, where women wore spectacular hats adorned with vibrant ribbons and silk flowers and voluminous gowns. then there's the modern world of today that yvonne designs for with styles that are both contemporary and a bit retro. if you're like me and love the mix of both past and present, you'll be entranced by *yvonne la fleur*.

covet:
wedding gowns
gorgeous veiling & bridal headpieces
carnival gowns
silk dresses
hand-embroidered lingerie
signature fragrances
custom millinery

notes

etc.

the eat.shop guides were created by kaie wellman and are published by cabazon books

eat.shop new orleans was researched by bonnie markel and dave mead, photographed by dave mead and written by bonnie markel, dave mead, todd van horne, tracy proler and robert, diane and gabriel markel.

editing: kaie wellman   copy editing: lynn king   fact checking: emily withrow
additional production: julia dickey

bonnie and david thx: not only our family and friends who reside in new orleans and make daily strides to rebuild, but also the countless people who returned post-katrina with the passion to bring business back to the city, and are doing so with a lot of heart and soul. and to kaie wellman, publisher of the eat.shop guides. thank you for allowing us the chance to explore, expose and pay tribute to the many wonderful shops and restaurants in nola. this book was no easy task but more a labor of love and the least i could do for the city i will always call home.

cabazon books: eat.shop new orleans

ISBN-13 978-0-9789588-7-9

every effort has been made to ensure the accuracy of the information in this book. however, certain details are subject to change. please remember when using the guides that hours alter seasonally and some-times sadly, businesses close. the publisher cannot accept responsibility for any consequences arising from the use of this book. the eat.shop guides are not advertorial. each business is chosen to be featured on it's merit.

the eat.shop guides are distributed by independent publishers group: www.ipgbook.com

to find more about the eat.shop guides: www.eatshopguides.com

PRINTED IN SINGAPORE